Helen

Val Benjamin

AuthorHouse™ UK Ltd.
500 Avebury Boulevard
Central Milton Keynes, MK9 2BE
www.authorhouse.co.uk
Phone: 08001974150

First published by AuthorHouse 3/13/2010

ISBN: 978-1-4490-7328-2 (sc)

This book is printed on acid-free paper.

Acknowledgement

Firstly, Gratefulness to God for this gift and secondly to my son Raymond Douglas for the hard work he has put in. Doing all the illustrations in this book, 23 years ago at the age of 12 back in 1986.

Also, special thanks to Joyce Asbury for her support to me during the production of this book.

By Val M Benjamin

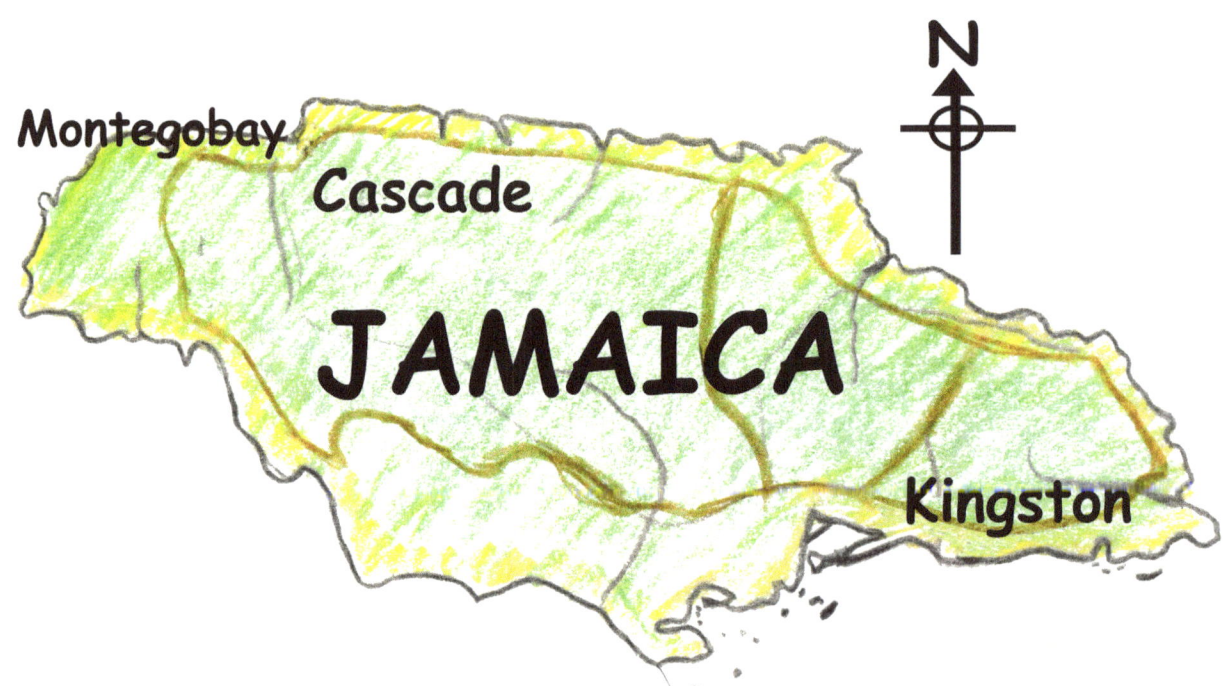

Montegobay

Cascade

JAMAICA

Kingston

N

MAP OF JAMAICA

Helen

Helen in Jamaica.

Helen is a 9 year old Girl, who lives in Jamaica with her Grandmother. Helen's Parents, two Sisters and one Brother lives in England. Helen was the proud owner of one Goat, three Hens and two Pigs. Each Day before Helen Goes to School, She has to feed her pets. Helen would also look after her pets in the Evenings after School. Helen's friend Mary, would visit her most Evenings to help her feed the pets.

One Day, Mary heard her Mother and Helen's Grandmother talking about Helen. It was very exiting what Mary had heard, so she decided to ask Helen about it.

Helen & Mary

Helen's Suprise.

One Evening whilst Helen was feeding her Hens, her friend Mary came shouting, "Helen, Helen, is it true?"

"Is what true?" asked Helen.

"You are going to England!" replied Mary.

"Don't be silly!" said Helen.

"W-E-L-L... your Grandmother told my Mother so," "I heard her when I was in the Kitchen!"

"Are you sure Mary?" Asked Helen. Mary nods her head.

Realy, realy sure?" asked Helen again.

"YES!" shouted Mary. Helen dropped the Hen's food and ran into her Grandma's Room, wi tears running down her cheeks.

"A wah do yu?" enquired Grandma.

"I - I", Helen was so upset, her Grandma was even more upset, not knowing what was wrong.

"Com on Chile, calm doun an tell me wah rang"

Helen & Grandma

Helens Suprise.

Garndma wiped Helen's face, and sat her on her knees.
Helen continued, "I don't want to go to England". Grandma starred in amazement.
"Inglan!... who tell yuh se yuh a go a Inglan?" asked Grandma.
"Mary told me so" replied Helen.
"Wah mek she tell yuh a ting like dat?" murmered Grandma.
Helen interupted.
You mean it's not true?" asked Helen.
"W-E-L-L, yes but mi did wahn fi tell yuh miself" Grandma replied.
Grandma began to explain to Helen why she had to go to England.

"Yuh si me dear, Grandma a get too ole nung, an yuh Modder,
Fadder, Sisters and Brodder a miss yuh in a Inglan" "Dem seh wen me ded,
no body will de de fi look afta yuh".

Helens Suprise.

"I realy want to go and see my family but I love you Grandma and I will miss all my friends, and the sunshine as well as my favourite fruits such as Mangoes, Guava, star apple and you know how much I love Suger Cane". "I couldn't bare to leave my pets...

Mango Tree

...and Mommy told me that they don't have Ackee Trees in England, so I won't get my favourite dish of Ackee and Salt Fish" Explained Helen, with her arms around Grandma.

Granma Assures Helen.

" Mi lub yuh to mi Chile, but yuh wi habb yuh family, yuh wi meet new fren an yuh wiget some different food" "mi hear se fish an chips is very nice" Explained Grandma.

"Will I get some Ackee and Fish?" asked Helen.

"Mi wi si weh mi can do fe yuh, mi wi sen som fi yuh wen mi sen a parcel, dem hab ackee in a tin so mi wi sen some fi yuh" assured Grandma.

Helen was very happy that Grandma isn't too sad, if she is she is hiding it very well thought Helen.

"I must tell my friends" said Helen. "Yes" said Grandma.

Ackee & Salt Fish

The Bus Stop

Helen's Journey.

Before Helen could go to England, she had to get a Passport, some injections and make some other preparations. Helen lived about 80 miles from the capitol of Jamaica (Kingston) where she had to go and get her passport and other things. This means that Helen had to get up early, about 5 o' clock, to get a Bus to go to the capitol. Buses only run three times per Day from Helen's town to the Capital, therefore, Helen could not afford to miss the early Bus. All this preparation made Helen feel rather important and she was very excited.

Helen has now been given a date when she would leave Jamaica. It was December the 22, just a few Days before Christmas.

"Yuh a go spen Christmas wid yuh family" said Helen's Grandma. Helen was even more excited. She packed all her favourite clothes as it was time for her to leave.

Helen's Journey.

Again Helen had to travel miles to the airport.

Her Grandma, Aunty, Uncle and some of her friends went to the Airport to say goodbye and Helen sobbed.

Helen finally boarded the aeroplane. It is so huge, thought Helen. As the plane got higher and higher, Helen began to loose sight of everyone. She finally stopped waving and began to think about leaving everyone behind. The air hostess realised that Helen was a bit sad, so she went over to her, gave her a drink and some food to eat. Helen, thinking that it might just be a few hours journey, asked "are we nearly there?"

"No" replied the Hostess, "you see Helen, Jamaica is 5,000 miles from England and it will take quite a few houres to get there, about 12 hours".

"12 hours?" enquired Helen.

"Just put your head back and have some sleep and the time will soon fly" assured the Hostess.

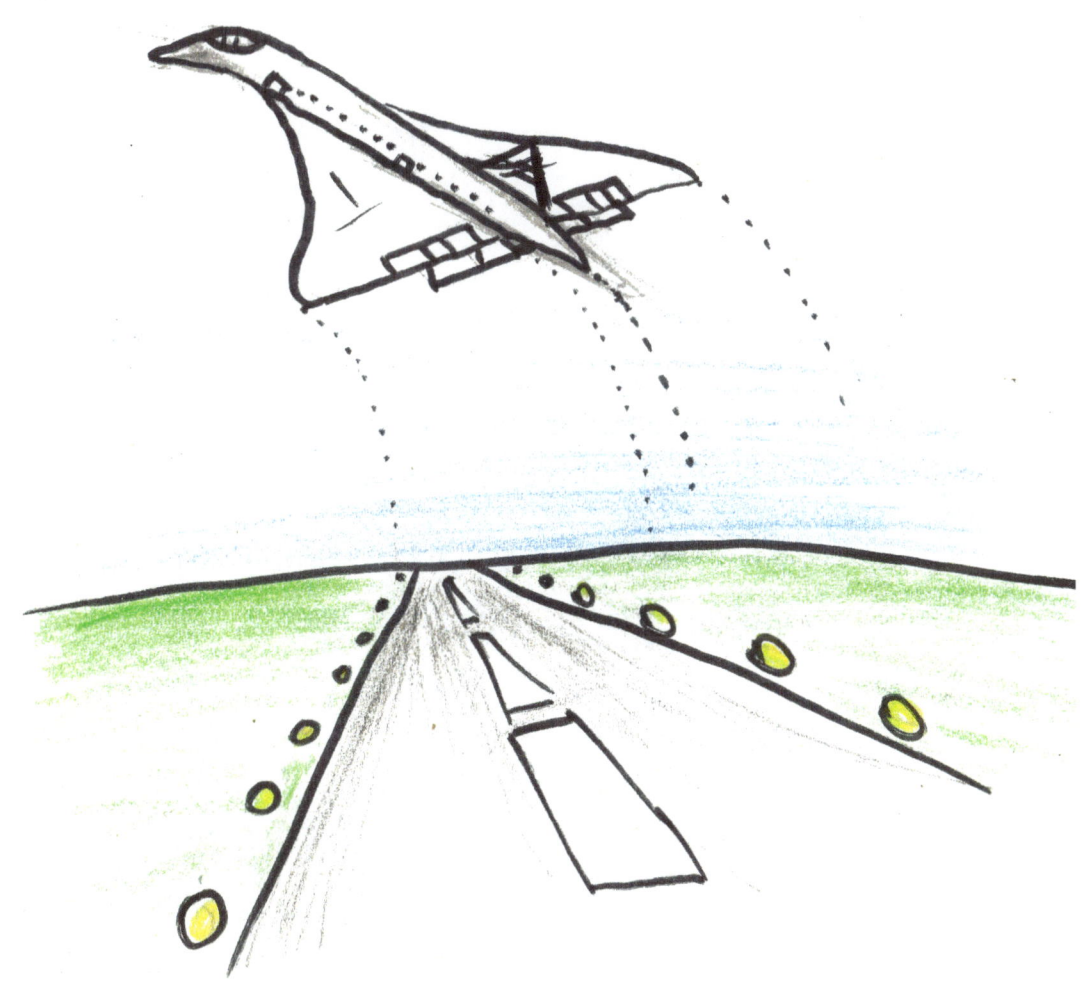

Helen's Arrival.

At last, Helen arrived in England. She was met by her parents, two sisters and baby brother.
Helen has never seen her sisters and brother before so she was very happy to see them.
Her family were equally happy to see her.
When Helen left Jamaica, it was sunny, so she only wore a summer outfit, but England was very cold and Helen's family had winter clothes on. Helen's sisters could not understand why Helen only had summer clothes on and Helen could not understand why they had on long boots, Gloves, Scarves and Coats. Although Helen spoke excellent English, she had a different accent. Helen looked amazed at the way everyone was dressed. She asked, "why are you dressed like that and whats all that white stuff everywhere?"
Sharron, Helen's 8 Year old Sister, Giggled, "arn't you silly... it's winter and the white stuff is snow, you speak funny" continued Sharron.

Tropical Fruit

Mango

Guava

Oranges

Bananas

Helen's Arrival.

"Sharron!" shouted Mrs jones (Helen's Mother).

"Be polite to Helen, she's not silly, she has never seen snow and it is always warm in Jamaica, some countries have different climates, customs and different food, so if someone asked you about your country it is not because they are silly" explained Mrs Jones.

On their way home from the airport, Helen gave Sharron some fruits and explained that she picked them from a tree in Jamaica.

"Why don't they grow in England?" asked Sharron.

Mrs Jones was the only one who had the answer.

"You see Children, these are called ropical Fruit because they are grown in a Tropical Country, A Tropical Country is where it is very sunny with no snow, just rain" explained Mrs Jones.

The children very excited that they had learned somthing different about another country.

Helen & Sharron
Pulling a Cracker

Helen's Party.

Everyone was busy preparing for Christmas, but Helen's family had some extra preparing to do. They were preparing a welcoming party for Helen.

Sharron's friends came around to meet Helen and all Helen's relatives were present to make it a very special occasion.

Helen has now started to settle in and adjusting herself to another custom. She has decided to write to Grandma to tell her that she is settling in.

Letter to Grandma

Dear Grandma,

      I had a lovely ride on the Aeroplane. It took 12 hours but I enjoyed the journey.
The hostess was very kind, she gave me some food which was nice. It is very cold in
England but I have had a new coat, some boots, some gloves and a acarf.
I now dress like my sisters and their friends and I am getting used to the food.
Sharron has Introduced me to her friends and I am getting on very well with them.
My family gave me a welcoming party and I had some mince pies, some triffle,
yorkshire pudding and some fish & Chips.
We took lots and lots of photos.
Here are a few of me and my family.

Love
Helen

www.ingramcontent.com/pod-product-compliance
Lightning Source LLC
Chambersburg PA
CBHW060820290526
45792CB00005BB/1738